The Alchemy of Butterfly Memories

By the same author

Poetry

Strange Beauty
The Poet in May

Inspirational

The Life of One

The Alchemy of Butterfly Memories

Olutayo K. Osunsan

The Alchemy of Butterfly Memories

by

Olutayo K. Osunsan

ISBN 1-4528-5354-1

All rights reserved.

Copyright ©2011 by Olutayo K. Osunsan

Copy Editor: Joneve McCormick

No part of this book can be reproduced or transmitted without written permission; violators will be prosecuted to the full extent permissible by law.

Poetry has afforded me the luxury of living many lives and exploring the experiences of various people, from presidents to paupers, and to develop a deeper understanding of people and life. And because of that I have been better able to understand myself, to heal and grow as a person: as husband, father, son, brother, and as a friend. I learned that everything will eventually become memories.

This book is dedicated to the voiceless and almost destitute...

Acknowledgements are due to the editors of the following publications, in which some of these poems have appeared:

Soul to Soul, Pyramid Magazine, Beginnings Magazine, World's Strand, Boyne Berries, Seam, In Our Own Words, Struggle and Poetry Arena.

"All human things are subject to decay, and, when fate summons, monarchs must obey." –**John Dryden**

CONTENTS

FORWARD..**14**

FOR YOU...**16**
The day you were born...17
Meeting..18
You are beautiful..19
Free...20
My daughter..21

BIG FAT WORLD..**23**
The publicist...24
Rebellion of the teaspoon poet..............................25
Promiscuity therapy..26
The matador..27
Lost...28
Tomorrow II..29
Streetlights..30
Music..31
Craving..31
Déjà Vu..31
The rain...32
On meeting a 'rich' brat..33
On being a fan (a.k.a. sh*t)....................................34
Waiting..35
Geisha...35
Temptation..35
I saw twilight...35

Destined……………………………………………..36
Kisaasi……………………………………………...36
Autumn comes……………………………………...…….36
Seduced…………………………………………...…..36
The heart…………………………………………..37
Like a dream……………………………………….37
Danish blues…………………………..……………37
Prostitute………………………………………….38
Butterfly memories………………………………..39
The truth………………………………………….40
Night………………………………………………40
Gypsy potion……………………………………...40
Heart broken………………………………………40
Fell in love……………………………...…………40
Regretting lover………………………...…………41
Beauty…………………………………………….41
Home………………………………………...……41
No smoking……………………………...………..42
A new beginning………………………………….43
Poet……………………………………………….44
Dying poet………………………………………..45
Songs of a new day………………………...……..46
The other woman…………………………………47

MIGHTY…………………………………....………**48**
Hero………………………………………………49
Nature……………………………………..……..50
Impossible……………………………...…………50
Illusive……………………………………………51
When great men go to war…………………...…..52
This is my place………………………………….53

BLACK IS BACK..**54**
I was born black..55
In Africa..56
Wendo (He)...57
The color of the soul...58
AIDS orphans..59
This is Africa...60
A wicked justice...61
Beauty in black..62
My fathers...63
The blue in black..64

LOVE IS ABOVE..**65**
I see the light..66
The anniversary...67
Dare..68
We got married..69
Distant..70
Letting go...71
Memory..72
My wife..73
You are divine...74
If love..75
True Love...76
I beg you..77
Trying..78
I have...79
Where you stand..80
Coexistences...81

10

The letter...82
Promise..83
Empty..84
Reconsider..85
Thinking of you...86
I chose you...87
Eduardo's Confession..88
Love me alone..89

NIGHT SONGS..90
Going home..91
Be near to me, O Lord......................................92
Trials...93
In my life...94
Intricate beauty..95
Sparrows and swallows....................................96
In love...97
The Lord's time...98
Broken..99
The Lord..100
Falling a thousand..101
Hiding place...102
Rebirth...103
Green mile...104
Mercy came...105
Lord you are..106
Righteousness..107
Hands..108
Seek..109
Sons of glory...110
Strong tower..111

I love you………………………………………..112
Praise…………………………………………..113
In his time……………………………………...114
In my room……………………………………..115
Judgment………………………………………..116
Our banner……………………………………...117
We will live…………...………………………..118
You always……………………………………..119
Salvation……………………………………….120
O Lord………………………………………….121
The darkness…………………………………...122
Songs in the night……………………….……..123
Rebirth II……………………………………….124
When the saints gather…………………………125
We love you……………………………………126
Save me………………………………………...127
Living waters…………………………………..128
God……………………………………………..129

THE DEEP END……………………………**130**
Dying…………………...……………………...131
Ready…………………………………………..132
The truth about life……………………………133
Kampala Road II………………………………134
Late one night………………………………....135
April's moon…………………………………..136
Light it up……………………………………..137
Paused………………………………………....138
Clock……………………………………..…...139
Lecturer……………………………….……….140
Difference……………………………………..141

Kill me...142
Insignificant..143
Life in a tea cup..144
Serving the people..145

FORWARD

I have searched my spirit as I search the street for an overdose of midnight gladness. It might cost, but still it will take me away from my pitiful self. – *from the poem Streetlights*

There have been, and will continue to be, many arguments over what constitutes good poetry; however, no one could argue that among the required attributes would be the maturity of voice, the uniqueness of perspective, and the willingness to bare the poet's most closely kept secrets, be they either of elation or of desolation.

I had the privilege of including Olutayo K. Osunsan's poetry in *The Other Voices International Project* over six years ago. At that time I encountered the work of a young poet who showed a unique eye but who was still growing into his life and his craft. His work, though technically sound, still needed the development that only comes with living and writing one's way through life. The structure of his poems, though solid, showed the awareness of one who was still too conscious of the poems that he was creating. The uniqueness of his verse was there, but one could hardly wait to see the depth that the experiences of living would add to his work.

In *The Alchemy of Butterfly Memories*, Olutayo has achieved that maturity. He skillfully weds these elements into a volume that is refreshing, distinctive, and mature. The craft of his poetry flows as natural as breath. He has journeyed through the trials and blessings of life, deepening his understanding of his way and the way of his words. As expected his faith in his work and himself has broadened the uniqueness of his poems. He pulls no punches, allowing the reader to view openly the joys and elations and the trials and tribulations that he experiences as a man.

In his poem "Hero" he says, *I am here to uphold justice*, which I find a fitting accolade to this book. Olutayo confronts life with no compromise in himself or his poetry. The world is portrayed, no matter the pleasure or the pain it may cause the reader and the poet, as it is, holding back nothing that he encounters or perceives. Perhaps the supreme quality of his work is shown in his ability to illustrate how we hide even joy from those around us, lest they come too close to our true selves. However, an even greater triumph is that Olutayo realizes that this is the ultimate mission of the poet, to allow us to recognize these deep held desires, longings, and satisfactions we all encounter in our worlds. In the mirror of his poems we all view our hearts exposed for who we truly are.

The book is divided into seven sections, each exploring a facet of life. The section that spoke the strongest to me was "For You", his poems to his daughters. This delicate side of pure love is too seldom explored in the works of male poets. There is a vulnerability but there is also a wisdom and strength to enhance the discovery of the fragility of being. In this section he brings us to that point when a man can look at his life through his child and finally "get it." For men we can read this and smile together in a solidarity of the completeness fatherhood brings. Women may read it and better understand the mystical strength added to a man at that moment, one he can seldom articulate, but can see reflected in this brave series of poems. Someday his daughters can read it and fully understand just what they mean to their father. Few men have ever had the fortune or talent to give their children such a gift.

I would like to salute Olutayo for this volume of poetry. His work makes our lives richer as I know the creation of such a volume has deepened his faith in himself, his life, and his words.

> Roger Humes,
> *Director,*
> *The Other Voices International Project*

For you

THE DAY YOU WERE BORN
To Bethel

The day you were born, I saw you,
Crimson like a wild flower yet to bloom.
Your white cry scraped the silence like a mute TV.

Naked and plump, you stretched your translucent hands,
Filled with blue veins, to capture invisible cords.

Your eyes shut in the light and still you blossomed
Like the radiance of the early sun, making every face beam.

My voice absorbed your bleached cry as you clung to my thumb,
With gentle pulses you shone on my silhouette like daylight.

I stared at your mother's eyes, because I thought you had stolen them,
The same way you stole my gaze and affection from the
moment I saw you.

MEETING

I only met you a minute ago and I already know we will spend the rest of our lives together under the refuge of the splendid blue sky. Our mornings will be crowded with unthinkable joy, our evenings with the delights of the universe.

All I need now is your name...

YOU ARE BEAUTIFUL

Dangling eloquently on the long neck of the sky,
You are the silver moon.

                                            You are beautiful.

Prussian pearls envy your eyes when they rise
With smiles of innocence.

                                            You are beautiful.

Seasons fade and life progresses into decay, but your beauty
Is here to stay like the undying light of the eternal sun.

                                            You are beautiful.

FREE

When the sun sets into its place, our dreams will be here with us, not chasing after the sun but here in our spirits; at home where peace reigns; where hope lives and joy will forever remain. As long as we fall asleep under heaven and angels smile down on the joy we find in simplicity, nothing else matters, but the voice of God invoking peace in our hearts, reminding us that the best things in life are free.

MY DAUGHTER
To Hannah

I
When I held your hand
The day you were born to me
Life made perfect sense.

II
Being your father --
Giving you life's very best
Just to see you smile.

III
Your translucent cry
And the warm pulse of your heart
Calls my name up to now.

IV
Each slow step you took
I stood behind with my heart
To guide your focus.

V
When you uttered 'dad'
I knew God knew me by name
And He favored me.

VI
My dearest daughter
To me you are heavenly
God's gracious love gift.

VII
If I ever fail
It would be because of more
Than I could endure.

VIII
And though years may come
When you doubt my love for you
Love never dies.

IX
A wife and mother
Still you remain my daughter
God's kind smile to me.

X
For you my daughter
My last breath will be for you
Just to see you smile.

Big fat world

THE PUBLICIST

Be the hero, the one that saved the world before breakfast twenty-four seasons ago.

The lunchtime millionaire who sold his bread in crumbs and made a fortune in an hour can be you.

If it is pity you want, I can brew it like fine Sunday evening tea and serve it in priceless china with affirmations.

The victor and the victim can be crafted and placed by dinner time. That will go well with blue wine and green-eyed monsters, under the lilt of Masai music.

Whatever you want, we can spin and twist the truth, as long as you tell me what you really want. I can always paint it grey if it is not white or black.

REBELLION OF THE TEASPOON POET
To my dear friend, the Poet

Coffee, very black, not filtered, is his choice.

Coffee-strained pockets of dreams
And a teaspoon full of talent.

Up till 2:30 am. Nothing, not even a drop.
Waiting for the muse. She never showed.

Searching the streets at awkward hours for her.
Maybe she offers night flowers. He'll pay for them.

At first his family though he was joking. Poetry?
The rebellious son of a poor man was final. A Poet!

Repent of your ways and get a real talent. A real one!

PROMISCUITY THERAPY

Mingling in the dark of night like two demons.

On garbage heaps, in abandoned buildings, alleyways,
Cigarette-stained motel rooms, on rainy car backseats,
And anywhere that the light of the moon will not find them.

Her skin: receptive, absorbing, consuming and embracing.

Her midnight ear always opens wide to listen;
With warm groans, aggressive clings and reviving embraces,
He buries all his burdens in her like a graveyard.

They part, absolute strangers again,
Into opposite sides of the darkness under the umbrella of mystery,
They fade till their next encounter a week or two from then.

THE MATADOR

Students gather for the last lecture,
Their oleaginous faces filled with colors of ambition,
Eyes intoxicated with dreams to fulfill.

All they need now is the endowment of a degree;
The last coins to make the piggy bank break
And pave the floor with gold and silver roses.

Some already have it, some don't know
And others know they just don't have it.
The end of the semester, the real world waits.

It waits like an angry bull exhaling pepper,
Ready to rage with the fury of blood red.
The outcome depends on the matador.

LOST

My daughter's sweet coughing laughter outside on the veranda, my pen chanting silent words on a pallid piece of paper, my mind far into the haze of inspiration; navigating the vulgar, illusive pathways of the mind.

                                                                                     I am lost.

TOMORROW II

Tomorrow the sun will rise; I will wipe the tears from my eyes and forget all the lies.

Tomorrow the clouds will make way, the blue will return to the sky and love will come back seeking me.

Tomorrow will arrive when it comes.

STREETLIGHTS

I have roamed the night streets till the lights weakened and the moths have retired. In my head, all the sad thoughts have made their way.

I have smiled at early morning strangers returning from sweat-drenched work. In my heart I always question the subtle madness of life.

How the sun rises without a second's delay for any soul or the moon departs without consideration for anybody's sleep.

I have searched my spirit as I search the street for an overdose of midnight gladness. It might cost, but still it will take me away from my pitiful self.

Searching for that speck of sense that will trigger a revolution in my world, an uprising in my spirit that will resist the urge to die slowly and silently as I cross shadows in the streetlight, night after night.

The night is my life of solitude; the streetlights are my sunrises, my transient hopes. The rest of the world is madness, subtle madness, and pure madness.

MUSIC

Music captures the heart,
Binds the wounded soul
And sets the spirit free.

CRAVING

A lion staring at the carcass
After the great hunt and the hush
And the stupid hyena coming to join
The feasting and perhaps become the starter.

DÉJÀ VU

Shy like snowflakes, you burn patterns into my head
And all I can do is see them in everything that is transient.

The lady walking by in the paper-bag suit under the
Palm of a damp umbrella shedding a fat droplet onto the pavement.

THE RAIN

Like a stranger, the rain comes naked and covered under the wings of the cold; its steps stutter at the windowpane.

The drops tap quietly at the window like a recently homeless beggar hesitantly asking for pocket change and trying to avoid the gaze of those who may recognize him.

The taps get stronger and the color of the rain turns cold with the bursts of the dust dying.

Sometimes it's magnificent the way the hostile drops kick away from the pane and head for the brown field to turn them green.

The rain is always a stranger left outside under the changing complexion of the erratic sky.

ON MEETING A 'RICH' BRAT

It's never too hard for a perspicacious individual to identify a parvenu with the elaborate expression that wealth is a *pas de deux*.

Every now and then even churlish stevedores can have the same appeal after claiming overdue pay cheques.

ON BEING A FAN (A.K.A. SH*T)

This kind of love starts like an insult spat at a passer-by on a busy Monday morning. It's one big filthy inconvenience. A bag of raw sh*t.

And so it begins like the story of pit latrines smeared in the mind, like the irritation of healthy purple flies on a pile of sculptured human waste.

That stupid feeling just won't leave and before you know it you are one of the flies and she is the sh*t. The tasty, alluring maggot-filled sh*t.

And other flies love her as much, if not more than you do. All you get are the songs, the pictures, the videos, the concerts, the magazines, the daydreams and finally the suicide.

When one fly dies, two or three others will take its place on the pile of sh*t. Sh*t is a big hit. Till the sh*t runs out. Sh*t happens all the time.

WAITING

Waiting like the *Koi*
For the oceans to expand
To spread my wings wide.

GEISHA

Lotus blossoms
Bloom with the smile on her face.
Lips of hot cherry,
Face powdered with the hand fan;
Poems pour from her dark eyes.

TEMPTATION

Cool trees that sing softly,
Healthy fruits that call your name;
Weary hunger yields.

I SAW TWILIGHT

I saw twilight
In the garden with a tree,
Its leaves dry and coy.

DESTINED

I smile at the dust,
My feet love its complexion.
Eternal cover
When I finally find rest
From the vanity of life.

KISAASI

Dust climbing the sky.
Debonair in my white shirt.
Late to work again.

AUTUMN COMES

3 She always cries
2 When autumn comes to a close
1 He leaves her alone

SEDUCED

3 Autumn sets her gaze
2 To undress the distant trees
1 Seduced by her voice

THE HEART

3 The heart is a house
2 Filled with restless hours
1 A house wife cleaning

LIKE A DREAM

Wrote a love letter
With the sad light of the moon
It was like a dream

DANISH BLUE

3 Royal blood runs through
2 The veins of a Danish blue
1 Till it is eaten

PROSTITUTE

She radiates within a corona like the fullness of a midnight moon.

Her innocent voice is disguised in guilt, seduction and insinuations.

Her night lips consume with the smell of money, mostly
when the sky is painted black with stars.

BUTTERFLY MEMORIES

Left behind
You feel like you are dying in the bitter fist of a withering flower.

The others are butterflies exploring the sweetness of freshly painted flowers.

All you can do is sing. Sing songs that give your imagination wings. The harsh reality is that you are still there.

In the decaying fist of a resenting flower in butterfly memories.

Forgotten by the future.
Remembered by the past.

THE TRUTH

3 For one very last time
2 Let me fight for the truth,
1 My death is certain.

NIGHT

Night stars discussing
A vast desert of darkness
The moon eavesdropping.

GYPSY POTION

Gypsy love potion
Fashioned by isolation
And the human mind.

HEART BROKEN

My tears called your name;
A tissue silenced them all
Then I fell asleep

FELL IN LOVE

3 I thought I saw you
2 In the green dress in the crowd
1 I always see you

REGRETTING LOVER

3 Yes, I lied to you
2 Every day is now a lie
1 Since I am not with you

BEAUTY

3 She sermons the day
2 Her eyes set in diamonds
1 All she sees are hers

HOME

3 The forgiving smell
2 Beckoning from a distance
1 Home's where I belong.

NO SMOKING

You tickle me with your tobacco words that cast smog in my lungs.

If the sky were gladly blue, your presence would tear it down
And light it up with fumes, like a chimney.

So, don't speak; better yet, don't come.

A NEW BEGINNING

Winds come in wearing the fragrance of spring, dressed in the rebirth of seasons, like a princess about to become a queen.

The rain is softer, almost eloquent, spreading out on the new green like soothing lotion calming beauty.

In the clustered sky, the sun is ginger and mild, melancholically tired but glad like the father of the bride.

With the change in season, a new beginning is declared.

POET

A heart full of poetry
And a blank piece of paper;
I am ready to challenge the world.

To pour tears in the drought
And grow wisdom on every plane.

My pen is my voice, the paper is my mouth
And these words are cleansed remains of my spirit.

Listen closely to the verse
Like the smell of sense,
Tea green in texture,
Truthful in complexion.

DYING POET

Feverishly I write this poem, like a lover's last letter to his beloved.
Inked in his blood, every verse is a stretching of my being:
A dying desire to be a poet whose words are the wealth of wisdom.

I write to let you know that poetry will never die, but I finally will.

SONGS OF A NEW DAY

In me dwells a brook of songs
A garden paradise washed by the sun
A beautiful world of handcrafted perfection.

When I cry diamond droplets kiss the earth.

In me is an undying season of happiness
The essence of simple beauty in flight
The voice of a million angels in chorus.

When I bleed viscous rubies adorn the ground.

In me eternity lives within every passing second
Waking in the morning to the glorious face of my wife
Hearing the gracious voices of my daughters at play.

When I die there will be no silence, just songs of a new day.

THE OTHER WOMAN

Peeling away into the distance
It felt like the scent of onions
In her eyes and she cried.

She hoped silently, like desperate prayers
To resist a beseeching sin;
The vibrations painted the house black.

She became a widow before
Her husband died, but she could
Not bury him. He still walked.

A younger lady with breasts like
Sun polished mangoes, barely ripened
But ready to eat, had stolen his mind.

She sat in the empty house, void like her heart,
Motionless, silent, cold and emotionless;
She sat there in a trance staring at the air.

The air was transparent and moved freely
Without restraints, feelings, hopes, dreams, or lost love.
She sat there, emptied of all her tears.

She waits for his return when the raw taste of mango
Starts to sting his tongue and causes rumbles
In his belly on a midnight bed.

At midnight when rumbles will not allow him rest
She hopes that his unsatisfied mind
Will wonder and find its way back home.

Mighty

HERO

My shoulders are pillars
My feet are foundations
I am here to uphold justice.

Throw roses at me and call me a hero.
Name your children after me because
It brings them good fortune.

But the hero in me is not the praises of the
Crowd or the awe in youthful eyes;
It is the sound of my heart growling in my chest,
The rumbling of blood rolling through my veins.

I was born a hero. It is my calling and legacy.
It is my destiny.

NATURE

I sat by the window waiting for her to arrive.

Nature's beautiful fury boils like an abyss.

She is temperamental as well as kind,
But you will never really know which is which.

IMPOSSIBLE

Driven by the desire of an impossible dream
Sometimes I feel like I am fighting the wind,
Pouring the majestic ocean into my pocket,
Trying to defy gravity and sense at once.

ILLUSIVE

Illusive like dreams running naked amongst times and spaces in confusion. Nothing is ever certain any more.

All that is left is hope.

                                                                         A distant hope.

WHEN GREAT MEN GO TO WAR

When brave men go to wars that cowards started
On broken fields thirsting for peace and crying for hope

When brave men go to wars that no one else is willing to fight
They stand tall, drumming their memories into history

When brave men go to wars under the shadow of a faded spring
Within valleys of endless remorse and waters of thick darkness

When brave men go to wars their spirits are polluted by death
And they sometimes see cowardice as a stepping stone to greatness.

When great men go to war, they go to protect what they love
Not to kill, eliminate or eradicate what they hate.

And they shed their blood like the brave, but never forgetting that humans die when killed.

They always remember that they can never afford to be a coward not even for a moment.

THIS IS MY PLACE
For Olukayode

This is my place among the titans,
Reinforcing the posts of the earth,
Carrying the world on my shoulders,
A mythological legend in my own right.

Sharks are born with fins
I was born with this.

Warriors only trust their swords
I only believe in this.

This is the optimization of my design.

This is my place of solace.

Black is back

I WAS BORN BLACK
To Africa with love

I was born black like the bottom of a charcoal pot.

I was born on the hard cold streets of murky souls;
Under the heat of the hateful lips of the African sun.

I was born black like angry boiling tar.

Forever cursed like a fishbone-leech tearing a naive throat,
Sucking healthy red blood and pouring black infested poison.

I was born black like an indifferent death.

Forever black like the undying night, unforgiving like a nightmare
And relentless like a vile disease only appeased by the mourning of death.

I was born black like deception, greed, lust, hate and even more hate.

I was born African like a shame, hidden, concealed, ignored, undermined and denied.

IN AFRICA

I
In Africa silence and sound are one,
The sun and rain do rein together
And we the people live and die at once.

II
The silence of thin rain droplets tiptoeing on tin roofs,
The sound of heavy women married for years
Weighing the weather to determine whether rain or shine.

III
Children whisper that a lion is being born somewhere
In the concealed secrecy of the African savanna,
Under the shade of an enigmatic tree surrounded by sun and rain.

IV
In Africa mighty kings are born when rain and sun clash
Over the footpaths and the tin or thatched roofs of tattered houses.
Shamba boys too are born under the exact same conditions.

V
In Africa everything meets; the past and the present,
Modernity and wilderness, old and young, today and tomorrow,
White and black, slavery and freedom, and of course
cultures.

WENDO (HE)

His song brings back the dying, right from the brink of the grave;
His voice is that of a lonely traveler cupped in nostalgia.

He sings of life and love and everything in between.

He never sings to the people, his voice is for their spirits,
Reminding them of what they had not so long ago.

Not much but enough to be everything.

When life was simple and dreams were not misleading shadows
Hiding in seduction amongst dark unfathomable objects of illusions.

We were simple then, we were proud of what we had.

Wendo sang along with the river current of the Congo
And his voice could be heard all the way as far as Togo.

He sang to our hearts and reminded us that best times are
Yet to come as long as we remember that our song is our
freedom.

THE COLOR OF THE SOUL

The color of the soul is hard to define:

I
The bareness of innocence right at birth, pure white illuminant cry that wakes all that is good, and the tiny warm clinging of its hand on anything it can touch.

II
The black death of a coarse soul, harsh like a pebble in my party shoe; silent, but painful like a needle piercing the most sensitive of flesh, inflicting misery one last time.

III
The knowledge that artists have the power to blend white and black in endless shades.

AIDS ORPHANS

Pack up the house, empty the accounts and auction all the children.
Tell them their father is no more, tell them he is dead.
Their heritage is the memories they cling to and the stories he told.
Let life be drained of everything, but sorrow. Deep heavy sorrow.

Their mother walks blindly into the future, hallow and fading,
Her days are numbered like certain famine after a poor harvest.
Soon her cries will be no more and all that will be left is silence.

Silence. Pure silence.

Silence like an eternity on a charcoal stove. Burning.
First the smell of human flesh, then the squealing of her spirit.

To the children, it's a nasty cut that can never heal. A cut
that can kill.

THIS IS AFRICA

This is Africa
Where he is them
And we are us.

This is Africa
Where the sun rises
But morning never comes.

This is Africa
Where promise lives
And hope died.

This is Africa
For you to see
But never to know.

A WICKED JUSTICE

I lived in a time when men valued money more than their souls,
Children forsaken for the sake of it and women were only leisure.

I lived when the rights of some were more important than others,
When giants stole from the poor and the rich just didn't care.

I lived under the saddened sky and angry sun,
The thinning ice and the crusty earth,
Under the veil of a wicked justice.

BEAUTY IN BLACK

The beauty in black is polished like black Italian leather shoes ordained to grace palaces and podiums of great heights.

It glitters like gold, stands tall and bold; precious like oil that runs a nation.

Blood-washed hands and tear-drained veins that still believe in the goodness of time and the quintessence of hope.

This is the beauty in black.

MY FATHERS

It was the blood of my fathers that trimmed the roads paved with gold.

They are their groans and cries that you hear behind the fading of every hearty laughter.

They are the voices that remind me, I am like no other, because I have to try harder and move farther to be an equal.

THE BLUE IN BLACK

The blue in black is that sad void that echoes that something is missing. Maybe black is less and definitely not blessed. History tells of it, the future predicts it. The nagging insinuation that poverty is a black man's disease and sickness is his bed of straws. *Billie Holiday* sang of strange fruits, but maybe they still hang on trees in minds of a dark continent's complexities. It's sad and it's blue because many see it as true. It's sad and true. But it's true: the blue in black is true.

Love is above

I SEE THE LIGHT

The wings of moths flapping against the light,
Casting huge shadows across the bright room.

Your voice

The irritating accuracy of time on a beautiful day,
Reminding you it will all end finally and soon.

Your words

And when the seasons stretch like a quilt on the line,
And nothing else satisfies, but the certain assurance of death.

The moths burn, the beautiful day ends and finally I see the light from the darkness.

THE ANNIVERSARY

A man at the bar taking two shots at a go with a melancholic smile written on his face under the tilted shade of tobacco smoke and darkness.

A woman, her beauty refined by her age, across from him shyly chuckles back to the absent soul.

She is thinking of their wedding.

He is thinking of his last affair.

Two decades and a year ago.

DARE

Fall in love with me if you dare and I will never let you go.
I have been captured by your ebony eyes set on caramel.

They pointed me out of the throng.
They set me on fire like nightfall on a lake, shedding colors with every move, promising the best is yet to come.

WE GOT MARRIED
To Judith

We got married in April when the hearts of the heavens were heavy with joy and bursting with such intensity that the thirst of the earth was quenched in a day.

We got married under the velvet of an evening sky before God and man, in temples built by God and one built by men.

We got married at the budding of flowers just before the procession of May arrived, before the voice of summer and the distant whispers of winter could be heard.

We got married after a journey of seventy-seven seasons of love, of doubt, of faith, of pain, of peace, of death, of birth, and of life.

We got married because of a love that speaks from the heart and not the eyes.

DISTANT

A star far into the heavens beyond my reach is your love, so distant into the colorlessness of the nighttime.

Like a phantom, I am never sure if it ever was or if it will ever return, but I am here waiting childishly with eyes abandoned in the night sky.

Wishing upon a star…

LETTING GO

It's easy letting go.
>But
>an
>eternity
>to
>forget.

I wrote you letters to explain how my heart pumps dust into the rest of my body; my soul is crumbling within me.

I wrote you endless letters, every single day of the year, but never mailed a single one.

Eternity must be filled with the shadows of your voice roaming in my head.

MEMORY

Drenched in hurt, my face is wrapped in crude-sadness. It's what love can do; tearing the feelings apart and making the world end with every fragmented moment, captured forever in the well of my memory. I chased the world but it was never worth it when love was lost forever in a sarcastic past. Love, look what you have done to me. I fell and landed in a thousand pieces, each still craving for the same person.

The same person, who has forgotten the smell of my hair, the sound of my voice, my first name and what I look like…

I cover each memory of us with a fresh coat of an ever-fading paint every single morning.

MY WIFE

Her smiles are like the stars in procession, one after the other they come and are never ceasing in magnificence or number.

Her eyes are the first glance of the most beautiful of mornings, leaving me craving for poetic words that are yet to be born.

The moon smiles down on me every night and I always smile back.

Her envy is my joy.
                My joy is my love.
                                My love is my wife.

YOU ARE DIVINE

You are divine; the stars dwell in your eyes.
Flowers turn to get a second glimpse,
The sun bows at your feet like the entrance of dawn.

My destiny was rewritten the day our worlds collided;
I knew there and then I would never live unless you lived
With me, by my side and became my wife.

Come away with me right here and now, again,
And I will devote every strand of my life to you.

New mornings and endless sunshines will always be there,
I will make the birds perform serenades to you alone,
You will fall asleep in smiles and wake with songs.

But you will never hear the same love song twice,
A new one and always better than the day before
Will always reveal how much deeper in love I will be.

The aura in your presence lights up my world
And I want my world to be illuminated forever.

IF LOVE

If love is fire, let it burn me with
Raging relentless flames, let it burn
True till I am crispy and no more juice
Dares to flow in my rustic veins.

If love is water, let it take me far
Away into the unfathomable depths
Of the grand blue ocean and bury my
Soul where it will remain lost forever.

If love is sand, let it swallow me with
Every grain, draining my spirit of doubt,
Let me be covered far into the belly
Of the bottomless, dark cruel lifeless earth.

If love is life, then let me live every
Nanosecond filtering the goodness
And the purity it spills. Let me
Never die. Let me die only to live
Again. And again.

TRUE LOVE

True love is a cry of the spirit,
It is de-winging an angel
And selling its voice into slavery.

True love never reasons much at all
It just listens to the shamelessness
Of the demands of the heartless heart.

True love is stupid and always the fool,
The one people point mocking fingers at,
In the mall, in the morning and at night.

I BEG YOU

By faith I have loved you.
A love that denies its power
To silence the restless spirit.

I have loved you with love
That speaks only with action.
A love that will always be found.

And by this love I beg you
To only love me half as much
As I have always loved you.

TRYING

Down this road many times
Like an addict heading to the crack house;
A struggling saint steering towards holiness.

Sometimes it seems like I am finally getting there.
Where it all comes perfectly together like a jigsaw.
I smell it sweet like honesty and taste the wholeness.

I open my eyes to nowhere; another perfect circle completed

And then I give up…
…for a while.

Sometimes for a very long while.

I HAVE

I have seen His face and touched His hands
And I know my Redeemer lives.

I have heard His voice and walked in His steps
I know that Salvation is here.

I have His Spirit and I am heading to the Kingdom
Now I know I am an heir with Christ.

I have the Kingdom in my heart,
Glory on my head and eternity in my soul.

WHERE YOU STAND

From the black fogs of Patagonia
To the white death of arctic frost
Through to the cruel heartless Sahara
That burns with the envious rage of a betrayed lover...

This relentless quest of mine will never end;
It will explore the breath, width and depth of my being
Till I find the very place you belong in this transitional life...

And finally I will give you my one true answer on where you stand in the equation of the alchemy of love.

COEXISTENCE

Words ran out three years back,
We are now just two memories
Roaming around in a hollow house.

Every promise that mattered is dented,
Smiles are lost, touches are repulsive.
We remain together because of habits.

Love might be holding its breath,
But I won't hold mine till it returns
Though I miss the taste of its fruits.

We grew together in and out of love
Into two separate paths of isolation
Splitting apart wider the farther we go.

Hating you would be better than this:
Knowing that in me there is a deep place
That forever remains vacant for you.

THE LETTER

My love,

Your words are wonders; they speak kindly like the embrace of the sun on a chilled winter morning. They find me every second of my day like fresh ink on paper.

They remind me that I belong in your kind arms, calm like the rocking of the waves wishing the shores well.

Everyday I linger from your presence; I reaffirm my resolve that you are the only one for me.

I will be lost always if we are not together like the interlocking halves of a cola nut.

I hear your voice at dusk and see your face in every thought, but like mist or a dream at dawn, it evaporates before I can reach it.

I am sick with love, blue with sadness and grey with depression; I wish time would pause so that I can steal a sigh from this despair.

I wish my memory would dry up like a riverbed at the peak of a callous drought so that I can forget you and for once smile at the sky with a complete life.

But I really wish you would read these frail words plucked from the gardens of my despair, in the autumn of my life and polished with the finest of hopes, that you might reconsider the love you once felt for me.

PROMISE

Promise me you will meet me there.
On the lonely road that leads to the tree by the river where we first met.

Promise me you will wear the green lace that reminds me of the meadow under the lilac sky in which we first danced.

Promise me you will wave when you reach the top of the hill. The way you always do on Friday evenings at my return.

Promise me you will smile when I hold your hand one more time as though we are walking down the aisle.

Promise me that you will promise never to forget how much I love you.

Promise me you will wait, even though you don't really have to.

Promise you will always remember us dancing.

Promise you will never forget me.

Please promise me.

Just promise.

Promise.

Please.

EMPTY

Empty like a drum
All I can do is hum
Your words still come

Some hum like birds
Others just like words,
But still they flood

My mind and everything kind.

I thought you left me behind

Still you are the one I seek to find.

RECONSIDER

I write you these verses with a heart of lead,
my eyes crimson like an irritated sunset
on the eve of the greatest despair.

Tears like shattered stars that once hung on a dream.

Sweet as the words may be,
their bitter core I pray
will haunt you till you reconsider:

My unreciprocated love for you

I am willing to take to the grave.

THINKING OF YOU

The universe
Your presence
The world
Your eyes
The sea
Your love
The day
Your light
The minute
Your spirit
The second

I close my eyes to die, I will be thinking of you.

I CHOSE YOU

When God shaded my complexion to compliment your presence, I chose you.

I chose you when destiny pointed at me and I took her hands to dance this dance of life.

The day I was born into the city where you are today at this very moment, I chose you.

I chose you with my first smile, my first step, my first word and my very first kiss.

Every sleeping hour, every waking moment and every living second, I chose you.

Choose me.

And I will choose you with my last dance, my last step, my last word, and my very last kiss.

EDUARDO'S CONFESSION
Inspired by a Latin American soap...

Camera. Lights. Action!

For you my love:
I will eat the coy petals of a thousand roses and then chew their violent thorns.
I will bath in an ocean of red sizzling wax, still boiling in the aroused fury of rage.

Just to have one dance with you.
I will paint a sonata with my Spanish guitar in the midnight air.
The stars will be jealous and angels will come to see.
To feel the touch of your gaze on my face, I will do anything.

Stay with me and I will steal you the heavens,
Sprinkle my heart on it and offer it as a token of my immortal love.

And...cut!

LOVE ME ALONE

Love is costly, yet simple enough for two to share.
Love is complex for three or more to comprehend.

Love eloquent, love gracious, love profound;
All that matters is that you love me. And me alone.

Night songs

GOING HOME

The silver cord is bent like a bow, ready to snap;
The golden bowl is a drought-riddled land with cracks,
The almond tree has found inspiration for its bloom in my hair.

In my house the two ladies strain to see through the tinted windows of my vision, my servants have halted their grinding duties, the strong men that carry the burdens are stooped low to their knees and the guards that are the pillars are trembling under the ebbing of time.

The sound of work has faded into the years and the doors to life's opportunities are shut; the water jar is already shattered and the pulley is broken.

Memories are left as tokens as the voice of the Master calls from his glorious abode.

BE NEAR TO ME, O LORD

Be near to me, O Lord,
Let my voice be incense,
Let it rise with approval
Into your presence with joy.

My heart beats under your wings;
Under the shadow of your name,
I will walk the valley of desires
And come forth as precious gold.

O Lord, nearer to you is all I want,
To a place where I have lost sense of self
And your voice is a song in my heart.
I want you more than I can ever conceive.

TRIALS

Morning shed its light on us;
Our words are few,
Our burdens are many
And our tears, unpredictable.

We are not certain if life found us
Or maybe we found life this way;
In a fix between hardship and character,
On a slope heading down to more.

God knows our hearts: the dreams, the desires
That come seeking His audience every morning
Before sunrise, while glitters crowd the sky
And our words sail heaven and earth for answers.

IN MY LIFE

In my life I have seen days that made me cry,
I have wished my eyes were draped in darkness
And tears have mapped my face with tributaries.

Friends have woven their fabrications into the gossip,
Family members have orchestrated my downfall,
And I have wished myself to be unborn to this life.

My smiles have been faked hundreds of times,
I have lied that it was dust in my eyes when I cried
And people have judged me by where I come from.

Poverty has erased the memories of my happiness;
Barefoot to school, kicked out of class for no fees;
I have cried under trees in my patched shorts - hopeless.

In my life, I have found a love that selflessly died,
Killed me and brought me to life in His loving arms
And still destiny tells me there are miles to go.

Miles to go before I rest; miles to go before I wake.

INTRICATE BEAUTY

Fragrance of your sailing voice
Spreads out like water pouring
Into my craving, thirsty eardrums.

And your beautiful face, atom by atom,
Crafted by God's magnificent hands
Through splendors and inspirations,
Heavenly revelations hidden in your smiles.

Your name is a journey into God's heart,
Tranquility subdues rebellion and doubts
And I start to believe in God and love afresh.

Who else can create such intricate beauty
That will drag time into a pausing awe,
A moment to meditate on His awesome majesty,
But God and God the Creator alone.

SPARROWS AND SWALLOWS
To mom

How pure and true is your dwelling place,
Where the sparrows build their modest homes
And the swallows release their shielded young,
By your altar, in your courts, in the sanctuary
Where your glory dwells and is revealed.

My heart yearns and even cries to be a sparrow
Or a swallow and dwell forever near your altar,
Leaning on your grace, gazing upon your face
And flying freely in your courts with songs.

Songs of adoration at the profoundness of peace
And devotion you pour into your creation.
For not even a sparrow falls without your knowledge
And in the palms of your hands you cup its soul,
Bringing it back with the kiss of love – of eternal life.

The young swallows call your name in the mornings
In anticipation of your visitation to their humble dwellings,
And how much more, I, made in your beloved image and likeness:
Craving and longing for more and more of you in my life.

IN LOVE

My eyes are set on you Lord,
You alone can take away my tears,
Only you know my regrets, shame and pain.

It is your strength that has brought me this far,
From the secret place to my mother's womb,
From my first breath onto this dying bed
And now it is solely you who knows
If my dry bones will live again to praise;
But Lord no one can declare your works
In the grave, nor can they praise if dead.

Lord you are my sunrise, the dawning moon
And everything in-between; you are my joy,
My hope, my strength, my best friend
And it is only to you I can call in pain.

I have no other God, but you alone.
At times my mind might have strayed,
But lord I am forever in your arms
And my heart is hidden in you, The Rock.

Here I am Lord, waiting for the mercy only you can give,
The grace only you can shed on my troubled soul.
I will lie here in my shame, here in my regret,
Here in my pain, waiting for your salvation again,
Because you never fail and your words are never in vain.

You are solid Lord and true. Forever faithful and just.
Abounding in mercy and surrounded by grace.
Lord my eyes are on your face, not your hands,
You will deliver me because we are in love.

THE LORD'S TIME

Mocking and scorning won't hurt me
It will only make me cling harder to you.
Stones and sticks will not kill me,
They will make me yield to your spirit.
All I ask is that you never leave me.

My eyes are hot with tears,
Shame is my blanket at night
And failure follows me on the streets
Letting everyone know I am with it,
But I am not moved, just waiting for your time.

My mouth is always damp with praise,
Worship brews inside my established heart
And adoration spills from my head to my toes.

Head high and shoulders square,
With my eyes focused on Jesus,
My feet on the path of righteousness;
I will go a million miles without doubting.

In your time you will make things flourish,
Days will be redeemed, tears will glitter joy
And I will be clothed in the royalty of holiness.

Goodness overtakes me, peace overcomes me,
Honor lifts me up and success is inevitable.
When the Lord's time arrives, it arrives in style.

BROKEN

Master, I know I promised
In thick or thin, good and bad,
Shame or fame, I will praise you.

Now Lord, I can't find my voice,
I can't pray not to mention praise.
I will stay silent here on the floor
Till you speak to my brokenness.

This heart of mine is too heavy to praise
And my tongue is in a drought,
But Savior, I will wait, wait for you
Here on the floor to find me crying.
Broken so you can pick me up – again.

THE LORD
To dad

May the face of the Lord smile upon you.
May his redeeming voice call your name,
His endowing mercy engulf your life,
And may his hands direct you.

For the Lord is good and faithful
And his thoughts roam amongst us.

May the breath from his nostrils revive you.
May his precious Spirit dwell within you,
His healing presence surround you
And may his footprints be your guide.

For the Lord is good and gracious
And his plans are for our children and us.

May the favor of the Lord our God sustain you.
May his heavenly hosts protect you,
His prospering revelations enlighten you
And may his essence go with you.

For the Lord is good and compassionate,
And his salvation is for our children's children and us.

FALLING A THOUSAND

Falling a thousand miles in love with you,
The roads paved with songs of adoration
Sending me to fall deeper every second.
Your affection
Your mercy
Your grace
Your peace

Falling a thousand ways in love with you,
The way the tree gazes and the sun smiles,
Giving me reasons to search and find you
Your voice
Your touch
Your face
Your words

HIDING PLACE

You are my hiding place,
A secret garden tucked in my mind
Where I go for soul-searching strolls.
Flowers dressed in dew,
Clear skies in shy blue,
Fragrant presence of you;
Tells me this love is true.

You are my comfort,
Where love songs are composed,
A place in my soul that dances.
Whispering candlelight,
Temperature just right,
My destiny in flight;
Your words just right.

REBIRTH

I place my cards on the table,
Lord you are more than able.

Everlasting God of heaven hear my cry,
Don't let my enemies rejoice while I die.

My spirit is poured out at your feet,
Master deliver me from defeat.

Unfailing are your mighty arms,
Save me and I'll praise you with psalms.

Eternal are the words of your lips,
I will tie your truth around my hips.

Peace-giver, peace reins in your kingdom,
Teach me your ways of great wisdom.

Provider, you are the champion of the poor
And the unjust are brought down to the floor.

Remember your uplifting promises for my life,
Let me die an old man in the arms of my wife.

GREEN MILE

Walking the green mile with a green smile
Is life's journey to its many deaths,
And for a moment insight beams into our hearts,
Realizing what we have taken for granted.

Every man has his journey to search,
Every soul, its lone moments to ask;
And for all its worth in our ungratefulness
We cry to God, 'Mercy! More mercy, please.'

When the green mile spreads before us to walk,
All we have left are memories, tears and smiles;
All life, a story: tragedy, comedy and romance
Plaited together into a sincere cord of reality.

MERCY CAME

Mercy came like any man would
In a molded fist of brittle clay,
Frail and able to fail every step;
With the ability to hate and curse.

They said God inflicted him
Because of his blasphemy,
But he is God and had no sin,
His only weakness was for sinners.

I am a sinner, the one he died for,
What my hands have done,
Where my feet have been
And things my mind had thought,
Kept him on a jagged cross.

Who will deliver me from the body of death

Mercy came draped in grace,
Bound by unfailing love to perform
In nail-pierced hands for my sake,
Nail-drilled feet dripped blood.

And thorn-stabbed head,
His white robe, crimson with sin,
Red stripes of bladed whips
Curved ridges on his back.

His eyes still had compassion,
The voice was still calling my peace
And his cry was for forgiveness.

Father forgive them, they know not what they do!

LORD YOU ARE

Lord you are my poem,
The song that rises within.
It makes me search for your face
Amongst the stars at night
To hear you sigh for me.

Lord you are my dance,
Tapping my feet to the rhythm
Of life in a searching crowd.
You are the master musician,
I am the dancer and life is the celebration.

RIGHTEOUSNESS

Blessed are those destined for righteousness,
Whose call is from the Lord our God;
The radiance of his face will reflect on them.

On my bed at night I meditated on your words,
In the silence of the night I called your name
And in my heart a new song was composed:

The song of righteousness in Christ Jesus,
Attained only by faith in the Spirit of God.

My self-proclaimed righteousness that was a filthy rag
Became blinding white by the blood of the lamb.

I do not live by the written laws of men,
But the Lord has written his laws on my heart;
It is now my nature in Christ to be justified.

HANDS

We all need hands to die in,
Arms that will remember the warmth
And the dampness of cooling tears.

Time rides on youth till it dwindles
Away into what could have been,
Our lives a journey rendered by the
Obstacles that try to carve us into
Who we might not want to be.

We need hands to guide us,
When the weight is unbearable to carry
And everything else really means nothing.

Our choices come back in hoary strands
Bleached by the seconds that mount into years
And moments that tried to define us
In selfless bouts of acts of redemption;
But hands that reach out for God's
Will cancel all wrongs and make us strong.

SEEK

In the house where you stay is where I seek
To sit and gaze where your glory dwells
That words will come and my spirit
Will interpret the deep longing in my soul.

I will call on you from here to the secret place
Where you knitted me in my mother's womb
And ordained me for praise of your holy name.

I will seek you in the morning, on the calls
Of the wind that search the whole world.

I will seek you at night, along with the hosts
In the heavens that stand in awe of you.

SONS OF GLORY

Lord God of all the earth
Everlasting king, father of all,
Our hearts are humbled before you,
For your name exceeds all generations
And your voice can be heard in all nations.

Setting the sun on wheels like a chariot,
The stars as spectators in this race
And we, the sons of glory, the centerpiece
When your angels present themselves before you,
They bring our praises, worship and adoration.

Though we might not be much to look at
Our lives are plagued with failures and flaws
And we are far from knowing our true heritage.

STRONG TOWER

My hands on the ground,
My knees on the floor,
Everything I hold dear,
Lord I place it right here
For you are my heart's desire.

I am yours for the taking,
And my life, I want to live for you;
In the good and bad times,
I will hold on to your name.

Your name is a strong tower,
A mighty refuge for the exhausted
And a home for the vulnerable.

I LOVE YOU

Lord I love you with a word.
A word that is unknown to man
That shakes my spirit with zeal.
A word that the angels contemplate
Out of its origin in man to God.
The word that is the summation of
My existence placed in your hands.
I myself don't know the word,
But I know it must exist in heaven.
Jesus I love you. Jesus I need you.

PRAISE

From the day of my birth, with my first cry
To the last day of my life, when death finds me,
Consistent praise is what you will hear from me.
Goodness that spills from you makes me alive,
Alive in praise amongst the living in nations.

Kings bow before you,
Generations seek you:
The refuge of the weak,
Strength of the mighty.

Praise belongs to you alone.

Those after me will praise you, because your goodness endures
forever and ever.

IN HIS TIME

The night. Sets. A clock. In. Seconds.
In. Minutes. In. Hours. In. days. In.
Dreams. Of Angels. At work in. The.
Presence. Of God on. The. Throne.

Presenting. Themselves. Giving. Accounts.
Of babies. Of children. Of youth. Of adults.
The angels. He assigned. Concerning. You.
Not a hair. Is touched. Without. Permission.

In my sleep. I hear Him. Call my name.
In adoration. I love. In care and concern.

Before I wake. The angels on guard.
My life on course. God in control.
In His time. It will come. To pass.

IN MY ROOM

His joy is a song my mouth can't sing,
It pulls me with it into His precious Spirit
And I can do nothing but fall on my knees;
His awesome majesty, the everlasting King
Is here with me in my room, on my knees.

I want to stay here forever, in this place
Where I can't find myself, just lost in Jesus;
His loving words surround like endless arteries.
More Lord, more of you, I want your love and grace,
To enthrone you alone in my heart for endless terms.

Lying on the floor in my room before you,
My knees tried, but they just couldn't hold.
In my tears, spread on the floor, an offering
To the simple things that amount to the great You:
Peace in pain, love in hate and faith in suffering.

JUDGMENT

Deliver me Lord from judging anyone,
Keep my eyes on my numerous flaws;
My only hope is in your salvation.
You alone know everyone's predicament,
Everyone's trials and tribulations.

Let my smiles be for those who stumbled
And rose again before they could be crumbled.

When I stand in your presence at the altar
In the sanctuary, at the place of worship,
When I lift my dry hands to heaven,
Vindicate me when people judge me
And my name is passed along the pews.

Let my humid heart do the walking
And my thirsty spirit the talking.

When I fall to the ground to worship
Let them know I did not do it to impress
Or in a religious spirit, but because my feet
Failed in the presence of your love and mercy.
Because my heart is soaked in love with you
And my eyes are blue in longing to go deeper.

Let my face light up with the joy of the Lord,
Because I have faith in you and your Word.

When the Day of Judgment meets us
And the books are unveiled in the grand assembly,
Every man will stand before the throne,
Motives will be made known and the Judge will rule.

OUR BANNER

An ocean of angels with swords drawn,
Arsenals, chariots of fire, armours of gold
And the Son of God, the captain of the hosts
Poised on his mission to save the souls of men
And place them in their rightful place.

Those who are with us are greater than
Those that stand opposed to the will of God.

Our heads will never drop nor our voices tire;
We will call on the name of the Lord our God.

The drums will roll and the battle cries be heard
And we will walk out victors and over-comers.

The battle is the Lord's and he will deliver us,
Because he is our banner before us.

WE WILL LIVE

Mountains are gray and valleys are green.
There are days and nights.
We will live.

Harsh suns burn the backs of those on the fields.
Rocks cut the soles of our bare feet.
We will struggle.

The baked earth crumples into dust as we plough.
Sweat and dreams water the earth.
We will labor.

Our fathers die in their struggle to find peace.
Our mothers cry in pain of lost love.
We will stand.

Blood flows through our veins when we are injured.
Tears fall from our eyes when we ask 'why'.
We will survive.

Stir down in our bruised hearts: *we will not die.*
Roam in our heads: *we will not hate.*
We will live.

We will overcome!

YOU ALWAYS

Too often my heart runs cold,
Your living words fail to inspire.
At moments my hopes feel expired.

Still, you always come...

At times my words sound quite hollow;
Promises I made to you never to fail.
And every so often I fall and realize I am frail.

Still, you always seek...

Sometimes this walk of faith weighs me down,
I feel too far away to even try.
My eyes turn moist and I start to cry.

Still, you always restore...

You came searching for my hidden soul
In the midst of a swelling crowd,
On the floor, in the tide, lost and alone.

Still, you always come looking for me
To see me through.

SALVATION

Write me a song,
A love song of lilies
At play in the fields of spring
And of emeralds, of diamond skies,
Of earth and heaven, where the divine
Meets desire and desire bows out to the divine.

It is all song. All joy.
By faith. By faith in Jesus.
Salvation belongs to our God.
This walk is too good to be true.
Hard at times, but never dull at all.
By faith. Not faith in faith, but faith in God.

O LORD

O LORD, at times I need your Spirit to call me,
The still small voice that brings tears to my eyes
When I am half way through orchestrating a sin.

Still you follow me in my rebellion to remind me
That I am not a filthy sinner, but a prince of God.

It's not a consuming fire or mighty waters that descend from heaven;
It's your goodness, mercy, graciousness and loving kindness
That sets my heart on fire and makes the spirit flow.

As far as my rebellion leads me, your spirit goes farther,
Hands that stretch from beyond eternity are to pull me back home
When I cry out 'O LORD' in my deep distress.

In my unfaithfulness you come faithfully to the rescue,
And I don't need to make the same mistakes twice,
I just want to do everything right to my possible best.

Though I initially shut my eyes to all your advice,
I will only listen to the directions you set before me.

THE DARKNESS

I'm the sound of the wind amongst the trees,
Whistling to the things that mingle in the dark;
In the darkness that has no discrimination,
That has no reservations, no sense of dignity.

We are all black in the darkness, without beauty,
Without pride or ego that drives us to rule others.
We are the same, slaves to the void that spoon feeds,
No one will over look or under look me in this thing.

In the darkness is a light that beats warm like heartbeats
In the hands of a murderer trying to redeem himself.
Elusive as it seems we hold on to it with all we owe
And the less we try the more it starts to shine.

SONGS IN THE NIGHT

Send me songs in the night,
Reveal your radiance in my dreams
And let the words of your lips
Meet my ears with vibrancy.

Set my heart on fire with songs
That my voice can never repress
And all the nations within me
Will call on your majesty.

This is the one thing I desire:
To love you with everything.

REBIRTH II

They buried me in their hearts,
They've attended my funeral
A thousand times and smiled
Over my grave in the dirt.

I am part of the dry bones
In the valley that is forgotten.

I am part of the mighty army
That the Lord is about to breathe.

Overcomers don't die; they fall down
And still rise, their eyes are on God.
Their strength is hidden in the Almighty.
They don't die, they live again to testify.

I am the brokenness, the nothingness
That the enemies see; the limping soul.

I am the rebirth, the generation.
The one God is rising for the last days.

WHEN THE SAINTS GATHER

Isn't it lovely when the saints gather
In the sanctuary, in the holy place
To call on the name of the Lord our God.

Their voice is the choir of celestial beings
That pulls a people closer to the divine
And invites the presence of God in our midst.

How glorious it is when healing flows
Like the oil of gladness into our lives.
God's faithfulness is our confidence,
Jesus' mercy is our eternal hope,
With the Holy Spirit, our comfort.

WE LOVE YOU

Our hearts rejoice at the name of the Lord,
We leap for joy in our spirits when He calls;
His voice is that of a perfect lover
Searching for his beloved amongst the vines.

Our smiles are priceless, they brighten faces;
We are so blessed to be called your own.
Your name inscribed on our souls
Is a pure gold medallion that beams light.

Our love- the Lord, our Prince- the King. Our all.
We clothe the ground you walk with adoration.
When the morning dawns you send forth angels
To lead us into our divine appointments – into destiny.

SAVE ME

My eyes search for the Lord,
Onto him I lay my petitions.
In a multitude of sins,
I call out to his Holiness
To save me from their grip.
Save me Lord! Save me I pray.

LIVING WATERS

My spirit speaks in the silence of murky waters
That flow through the streets of my being.
They can't be compared to the springs of living
Waters that flow from you, and I seek
To be cleansed by your purifying touch
That in me there might be a fountain of living waters.

GOD

God is the castle in which I live,
The mighty one who shoulders my world;
The song that transforms my fleeting being.

The sunlight of His eyes, the breeze of His voice,
The strength of His touch and the might of His will.

God is the dream in which I live,
The everlasting colors that chronicle my minutes;
The nebula that clothes me with subdued radiance.

The deep end

DYING

An orphan searching for the last trace of a parent,
My heart coughs blood in its rage
And here I lie: a dying soul
With only hope remaining.

Death, like life, is a journey of self discovery;
Every dying breath is one more surprise and a mystery.

Here I lie: a worthless child of nobody,
Dying in the core of a crowd of the living,
And no one can spare me an ounce of life.

Lying here, everything so clear
Like my mother's washed crystal ware:
Illuminating everything next to it.

Everyone is learning from my dying:
Life is simple at the end of it all.

Close your eyes and sigh

READY

Shadows that fall on golden leaves sending thoughts of decay...
Today could be the day, or maybe tomorrow;
In every way, I am ready as a clock
Ticking for every second, minute or hour.

THE TRUTH ABOUT LIFE

The truth about life is.

Some people's hunger for death exceeds their thirst for life.

They take a bite first. Mouthful. Nibble. Whatever.

The truth about life is that you die when you live.

You live when you die.

And dying, like *Sylvia*, is an art.

Not all people do it well.

KAMPALA ROAD II

Here gas. There gas.
Everywhere teargas.
Don't ask.
Just run.

Here mamba. There mamba.
Everywhere black mamba.
Don't ask.
Just run.

Human dignity is nothing here?
Stand and find out if you dare.
Don't ask.
Just run.

LATE ONE NIGHT

Late one night on my way home
I stood at a junction on a dark street
To forge a reason for my life.

For an hour or more I stood like a streetlamp
Illuminating the darkness within me
And it finally came to light that I was drunk.

Like a mule stacked high with burdens
I made up my mind to return at daylight
When impatient cars will end all my questions.

APRIL'S MOON

April's moon is shy like a newborn's voice.
The emerald hills, ruby skies and diamond
Lakes shrivel into golden fields and silver skies.

Even the lilac breeze remains no longer at ease;
She tiptoes into the folds of the earth like a thief.

April's moon is like no other in the twilight,
It shuts the eyes and slows the breath
Till there is only silence under the night.

LIGHT IT UP

Light it up;

Set it on fire
Let it take you higher
Till you are up on the wire
Hanging by your chimney neck
With your cool life a massive wreck
And an expensive habit too late to check.

Remember to smile like a star,
Always share what you got at the bar
And never ever talk about its miserable scar.

PAUSED

My life is a dirty khaki file on the desk of a big man…to be approved, rejected or maybe stamped pending. Everything I have ever done is summarized on one quarter of an A4: "he'll take leaves and see his children graduate from college before he decides…then his moods will dictate my future."

Till then I will pause my life, keep my dreams and bury my ambitions.

CLOCK

I think when I walk
My brain ticks and talks
As I walk like a clock.

                                          Tick think, talk talk.

I talk when I think
Like a clock I tick
I tock with words.

                                          Tick talk, think talk.

LECTURER
To the fickle minded

The lecture hall is cold, hard and grey;
The least likely place to find a prey.
But knowledge burns softly in blue
And everything the lecturer says is true.

F-

She will give the angel a smile to borrow
And ponder about the wonders of tomorrow
When they will relate under the disguise
Of two consenting adults and all will suffice.

A+

DIFFERENCE

Happiness and death. Sorrow and celebration.
Strangers and separation. You and I
One and the same. Relevant and useless
What difference does anything make.

KILL ME

Like an expensive Cuban cigar crushed in a crystal ashtray,
You kill me and my spirit rises in a room in light translucent white.

Twisting and turning, I faded into nothingness,
A stranger walking away into the peach shadow of a lost night.

"You kill me," I called out in a foreign tongue to a room
Blind, deaf and mute with red tapes and bureaucracy.

When I wake up every morning the big man frustrates me
Again and again and again, because I don't matter much.

You kill me. Why don't you just kill me?

Kill me!

INSIGNIFICANT

Insignificant I must be.
You shine like a supernova.
I like a dim damp spark,

Only seen through blind gazes of those who stare at you.
A dark spot in the light.
Fleeting.
Minute.
Insignificant.

LIFE IN A TEA CUP

My entire life is in your tea cup.

Sometimes you sprinkle sugar
other times you stir viciously.

But at the end of it all you take
a gulp and spit it all on the floor.

SERVING THE PEOPLE

An ego thrice his size
Won the election by selection.

Sits in a false ivory tower,
Barking at the miserable 'dogs'.

A flashy suit. Uncultured.
Taste for tacky women- married or not.

German cars. Italian design.
French wine. Heavy African accent.

Swiss accounts. American mansions.
Domestic 'slaves'. Handpicked imported friends.

Loves Africa. Hates African.
Believes in Jesus, Allah, Buddha and 'the ancestors'.

Misallocating donor resources for the people.
Sweaty crumpled notes at their service to dig potholes.

Made in the USA
Columbia, SC
10 November 2024